DEVOTIONAL

How to Hear God's Voice

DEVOTIONAL

How to Hear God's Voice

SARAH WEHRLI

FO
UR

My heart has heard you say,
"Come and talk with Me,"
and my heart responds,
Lord, I am coming.

Psalms 27:8 (NLT)

CONTENTS

CHAPTER 1

THE PROMISE OF HEARING

Call to me and I will answer you, and I will tell you great
and mighty things which you do not know.
Jeremiah 33:3 (NASB)

Growing up, I heard my dad, a pastor, teach often about hearing from God. Through examples from the Bible and his own personal experiences, he showed us that hearing from God isn't just for pastors and religious leaders. It's for everyone! If you know Him, you can hear Him. This truth produced a deep passion in me to truly *know* God—to build an intimate relationship with Him. Still, as I processed this, I had questions. Questions like, *What does God sound like? And how will I know it is Him?*

I received some answers to these questions when I was 11 years old. I was in a worship service at church, singing with my hands lifted high. As I worshipped, I heard a voice speaking to my spirit, and I immediately knew it was God. For a few minutes, He showed me some of His plans for my future and made clear a cause to which He wanted me to give my life. That experience marked me. I had proof then that God still speaks—and not because He has to speak. He *wants* to speak. In that moment, I felt His love and sensed His longing to lead all of His children into His beautiful purposes.

If you are reading this, you might be where I started. You likely want to hear from God, but you have questions. I want to begin our time together by answering one of those questions for you as clearly as possible. This answer is not only based on Scripture; it's also based on experience. God *still* speaks to His people. You *can* recognize His voice. Jesus said in John 10:27, "My sheep hear my voice; I know them, and they follow me."

THE PROMISE

All throughout Scripture, we find examples of men and women who learned to hear and follow God's voice. In the Old Testament, we read about people like Abraham, Moses, Joshua, Samuel, Deborah, Elijah, Isaiah, Jeremiah, and Daniel. In the New Testament, we read about people like Paul, John, Peter, Philip, and Cornelius. The best part is they were all regular people like you and me.

We not only find *people* that prove this reality; we find more *promises* that prove it, too. In Isaiah 30:21, we're promised, "Whether you turn to the right or to the left, your ears will hear a voice saying, 'This is the way; walk in it.'" Proverbs 3:5-6 (NKJV) says, "Trust in the Lord with all your heart, and lean not on your own understanding; in all your ways acknowledge Him, and He shall direct your paths." In Isaiah 58:11 (NLT), we read, "The Lord will guide you continually."

You might think, *But Sarah, I don't think these promises apply to me. I am a follower of Jesus, but I've messed up too much.* Or maybe you think, *I haven't followed Jesus long enough. I could never recognize His voice!* Let me shine light on this truth for you today: these are lies of the enemy to keep you from hearing God, obeying Him, and building the life He has called you to live. If you have accepted Jesus, you *can* hear from the Lord. His Spirit *will* lead you.

Friend, you're not on earth by accident; you're here on purpose and for a purpose. And this purpose is not just something God threw together last-minute; He planned it from the beginning of time. Ephesians 2:10 (ESV) says, "For we are his workmanship, created in Christ Jesus for good works, which God prepared beforehand, that we should walk in them."

God *still* speaks to His people.
You *can* recognize His voice.

THE PROCESS

Now that we know the promise of hearing from God, let's talk about the process. There are two steps in following God's plan for our lives: hear and obey. Matthew 6:33 (NKJV) talks about the first one when it says, "But seek first the kingdom of God and His righteousness, and all these things shall be added to you." Jeremiah 29:11-13 says, "'For I know the plans I have for you,' declares the Lord, 'plans to prosper you and not to harm you, plans to give you hope and a future. Then you will call on me and come and pray to me, and I will listen to you. You will seek me and find me when you seek me with all your heart.'" Matthew 7:7 says, "Ask and it will be given to you; seek and you will find; knock and the door will be opened to you."

In these passages, we see that seeking God is not an arduous task. Why? Because He *wants* us to find Him! He wants us to hear from Him and then obey Him, building the life He has destined for us.

I was reminded of the importance of both steps in this process when we built our home a couple years ago. On the first day, the contractor didn't simply show up and start laying concrete. First, we met with the architect, and he designed a blueprint that fit our specifications. He carefully planned every aspect before he was ready to bring our dream to life. Then, the contractor started building, following the plan closely. The process took time, but the result was worth it!

It's the same in our lives. Our Master Architect has already drawn the perfect blueprint for us. Our job is to spend time with Him, receiving His plans. Then we are to take steps of faith to build. The process may feel long, but the result will prove more than worth the work. It's important to note though, that, unlike building a house, when building our lives, God doesn't let us see the whole blueprint at once, because it would likely overwhelm us. Instead, He guides us step by step. As we seek Him, He reveals our next move.

Now, I realize not all of us are new to hearing from God. You might read this not wondering if you can hear Him, but wondering why you haven't heard Him lately. If that's you, I encourage you to ask yourself: how many voices are vying for your attention? How many opinions are you giving weight to right now? Think of hearing God like finding a specific station on an old-fashioned radio. When you search for that station, you must tune past a lot of static to get there. But when you finally do, it's beautiful. The static is gone, and the music is clear.

It's the same with hearing God. In order to hear clearly, we must tune past the static of all other voices, opinions, opportunities, and distractions. When we do, His signal will be loud and clear.

So now, we've discussed both the promise and the process of hearing God's voice. We know that the guidance of His Spirit is available to all who know Him. In the next chapter, we'll talk about the ways God speaks. Are you ready to continue? Remember—God loves you. His plans for you are good, and you *can* hear His voice.

You're not on earth by accident; you're here on purpose and for a purpose.

Questions for reflection:

1) Have you ever heard God's voice? If so, when? Write about your experience.

_____

_____

_____

_____

_____

_____

_____

_____

_____

_____

2) What are some questions you have about hearing from God? Write them out, and as you continue through this devotional guide, return to record the answers you find.

_____

_____

_____

_____

_____

_____

_____

_____

_____

3) What lies are you believing that could hinder you from hearing God? If you don't know, pray about it. Ask the Holy Spirit to reveal them to you. Then, write these lies out, and find a correlating truth from Scripture revealing God's promise. Anytime you start to believe one of those lies, return to these verses, speaking them over your mind and heart.

_____

_____

_____

_____

_____

_____

_____

_____

_____

_____

_____

_____

_____

_____

_____

_____

Passage for further study:

Isaiah 55

Prayer for today:

Father,
I come to you in the name of Jesus, desiring to build a relationship with you.
As I do, I believe I will hear your voice. As I acknowledge you, please direct
my steps. Show me things to come. Give me a discerning heart and help me
refuse the lies of the enemy, filling me with the knowledge of your will.
In Jesus's name,
Amen

CHAPTER 2
THE WAYS GOD SPEAKS

*Those who do not believe God speaks specifically will simply ignore or
explain away all the times when God does communicate with them.
However, those who spend each day in a profound awareness that
God does speak are in a wonderful position to receive His word.*

AW Tozer[1]

After my encounter with God at 11, I continued to serve Him and even hear from Him occasionally. I attended church regularly and always tried to do the right thing. But it wasn't until I was 14 that things really clicked for me. It was then I began desiring a genuine relationship with my Heavenly Father, committing to put Him first in everything.

It all started at youth camp. During one worship service, the Lord asked me, "Sarah, am I first in your life?"

I thought about it for a minute. Then, I responded, "Well, sure, Lord. I am a good person. And you know I love you."

He said, "No, Sarah. Am I your *best* friend?" I thought for a minute again. Though I didn't want to admit it, I knew my answer was no.

Sure, I had accepted Jesus as my Savior when I was young. I knew much about God, and after my encounter at 11, I had begun to hear His voice. But truthfully, He wasn't first in my life. I didn't really even have a friendship with Him. In fact, as I looked down the row of seats at all my friends sitting next to me, I realized

I cared more about their friendship than I did about His. It was then I realized: I couldn't ride on my parent's faith anymore; I had to make my faith my own.

> ## "You will seek me and find me when you seek me with all your heart." —Jeremiah 29:13 (NIV)

In that service, I surrendered my life to Jesus afresh, resolving to build our friendship. When I returned home, I began spending consistent time with Him. I found a Bible that was easy for me to understand and a devotional that taught me how to study His Word. I started getting up early before school to read His Word and pray. What started out as a 15-minute period slowly grew. I started looking forward to this time with God. I asked Him to make His Word come alive to me and to speak to me daily, and He did! I began receiving wisdom and insight from Scripture and recognizing His leading through prayer. It was amazing! As I continued to spend regular time with Him, He truly became my best friend.

Throughout high school, I continued to put God first in my life. The more I sought Him, the more our relationship grew. The more our relationship grew, the more He spoke. And the more He spoke, the more comfort, clarity, and direction I received for my life. Now that I'm older, I realize building a relationship with God is vital to hearing from Him, and hearing from Him is one of the most important things we could ever learn to do.

Perhaps that's why hearing/listening is talked about so much in Scripture. The Bible mentions the word *love* 490 times and the word *faith* 250 times. It mentions the word *talk* 160 times, but it mentions the words *hear* and *listen* 678 times.[2] Obviously, all of these words are important, so why is *listen* mentioned so much more often? Probably because it covers everything else! When we listen to God's voice, then obey it—we walk in love, faith, and purpose.

God created you. He knows exactly how to speak to *you* so that you best receive and understand His heart and His plans.

One of my favorite stories about hearing from God is the story of Samuel in 1 Samuel 3. At the time this story took place, Samuel did not yet have a relationship with God, but he worked under Eli, the priest, and lived in the temple. The chapter starts by telling us that, "In those days the word of the Lord was rare; there were not many visions." But one night, Samuel was lying down when the Lord called him. Samuel, thinking it was Eli, went to Eli and said, "Here I am. You called me." Eli responded, "I did not call. Go back and lie down."

This happened twice more before Eli realized what was happening. In verse 9, he told Samuel, "Go and lie down, and if he calls you, say, 'Speak, Lord, for your servant is listening.'" Samuel obeyed. When he listened, God revealed His plans to him. From then on, Samuel started building his relationship with God. As he did, God continued to speak to and lead him. The process is the same for all of us. As we build our relationship with God, He will speak to us, too—and in more ways than one.

That's what we're going to talk about in this chapter. In the last chapter, we discussed the promise of hearing God. Now, I want to talk about the ways in which He speaks. The longer you follow God, the more you'll realize: though God speaks to us all, He doesn't speak to us all in the same way. So, as we discuss the various ways He speaks, don't feel discouraged if you find one you haven't encountered yet. Rather than comparing yourself with others, remember that

God created you. He knows exactly how to speak to *you* so that you best receive and understand His heart and His plans.

HIS WORD

The first way God speaks to us is through His Word. 2 Timothy 3:16 (ESV) says, "All Scripture is breathed out by God and profitable for teaching, for reproof, for correction, and for training in righteousness." We can read Scripture with confidence that comes from knowing that it contains God's words. Psalm 119:105 says, "Your word is a lamp for my feet, a light on my path." The Word illuminates things in our hearts. It reveals His truth to us, and it directs our steps. John 1:1 says, "In the beginning was the Word, and the Word was with God, and the Word was God." Jesus was The Word made flesh. So, if we want to know Jesus, we must know Scripture. If we want to hear His voice, we must prioritize His Word.

James 1:23-25 says that God's Word is like a mirror. It shows us who we are in Christ and highlights the areas in which we need to grow. It speaks to our potential—to who God made us to be. It is also like a sword. Hebrews 4:12 says, "For the word of God is alive and active. Sharper than any double-edged sword, it penetrates even to dividing soul and spirit, joints and marrow; it judges the thoughts and attitudes of the heart." We have a soul (our mind, will, and emotions), we live in a body, and we have a spirit. We need discernment to know out of which part we're operating, and that's what God's Word does. It divides.

Matthew 4:4 says that God's Word is like food for our spirit. 1 Peter 2:2 says that it's like a baby's milk, nourishing us and helping us grow. We hunger for whatever we feed on, so as we continually fill ourselves with God's Word, our hunger for it will increase. John 8:31 says, ". . . If you hold to my teaching, you are really my disciples. Then you will know the truth, and the truth will set you free." The Word is not just another self-help book. It has the power to transform our hearts and lives forever!

What I love most about the method of hearing God through Scripture is that it is one-hundred-percent reliable. It's also a solid measuring stick for when we feel we've heard Him another way. Everything God speaks should line up with

His Word. The Word is our ultimate authority. Elisabeth Elliot said, "The Bible is God's message to everybody. We deceive ourselves if we claim to want to hear His voice but neglect the primary channel through which it comes. We must read His word. We must obey it throughout our lives."[3]

The Word is not just another self-help book. It has the power to transform our hearts and lives forever!

HIS VOICE

The second way God speaks to us is through His Holy Spirit living inside of us—His still, small voice. John 16:7-14 (AMP) says:

I tell you the truth, it is to your advantage that I go away; for if I do not go away, the Helper (Comforter, Advocate, Intercessor—Counselor, Strengthener, Standby) will not come to you; but if I go, I will send Him (the Holy Spirit) to you [to be in close fellowship with you]. And He, when He comes, will convict the world about [the guilt of] sin [and the need for a Savior], and about righteousness, and about judgment: about sin [and the true nature of it], because they do not believe in Me [and My message]; about righteousness [personal integrity and godly character], because I am going to My Father and you will no longer see Me; about judgment [the certainty of it], because the ruler of this world (Satan) has been judged and condemned. But when He, the Spirit of Truth, comes, He will guide you into all the truth [full and complete truth]. For He will not speak on His own initiative, but He will speak whatever He hears [from

the Father—the message regarding the Son], and He will disclose to you
what is to come [in the future].

As Jesus prepared to leave earth for heaven, He promised believers the gift of the Holy Spirit, whom He called the Helper. The Holy Spirit wants a close relationship with you. He wants to comfort you, direct you, and encourage you. Sometimes the Spirit speaks specific words, and sometimes He speaks through an indescribable knowing. With the latter, you may feel you simply know the right decision to make when you pray, though you may not understand why. The Holy Spirit speaks to us in both ways, and it's important to honor both.

When you first hear the Holy Spirit, you might wonder if what you're sensing is really just the leftover pizza you ate for dinner! But it's like any relationship. Spending time with someone causes you to recognize their voice more easily. When my husband calls me, he doesn't have to introduce himself. We're in an intimate relationship, so I know it's him right away. The same thing happens when we pursue a continuous relationship with the Holy Spirit.

Everything God speaks should line up with His Word. The Word is our ultimate authority.

Often, when we spend time with the Holy Spirit, He will prompt our hearts to pray for certain things. I'll never forget the day I first experienced this. I had been praying before school when the Holy Spirit prompted me to pray for a girl in my class. Later, I found out she was in a terrible car accident that morning. Her car was destroyed, and it was a miracle she was alive. I was thankful for her safety and for the confirmation that I had truly heard God.

Many people say they hear the Spirit most clearly when in worship. We're especially tuned in to Him during that time, so it can be easier to receive heavenly downloads from Him. One day, this happened to me during a church service after I uttered the same prayer I have for years—the one Samuel prayed. I said, "Lord, I feel like I'm doing what you've called me to do right now, but if there's anything else you desire for me to do, I am yours. Here I am, Lord. Speak to me."

In the past, when I prayed this, I hadn't always received new direction. Sometimes, I simply had been given confirmation I was on the right track. This day was different, though. The Holy Spirit spoke to me—and to be honest, I was shocked at His request.

He asked, "Sarah, would you be willing to move to the mission field for the next season of your life?" We had been involved in short-term mission trips, but I had not thought about moving overseas at that time in my life. My husband Caleb and I were in the busiest season of our lives until that point. We had a toddler, and I was pregnant with our second child. We had just bought a house, which we'd believed God for since we had gotten married. The college ministry we were leading at our church had just started experiencing tremendous growth. We were happy and fulfilled and certainly not looking for change!

I reminded God of these things as if He didn't already know. He responded, "Sarah, if you don't step out into this new thing I'm calling you to, then you won't reach the people I've called you to reach. You'll grow stagnant in your faith. You'll also hinder other leaders you've been preparing, and you'll hinder the future of this college ministry."

I knew I didn't want any of that. I wanted to obey. So although there were still a lot of unknown factors, I gave God my yes. As worship concluded, I thought about how I would explain what I heard to Caleb. I ended my prayer of commitment with, "But God, please tell my husband. I don't want to be the one persuading him to do it."

Thankfully, God likes to confirm things. When I went home that night, Caleb asked, "Sarah, what is God speaking to you? I know He is speaking to you." I didn't want to tell him, but he kept asking. Finally, I gave in, prefacing it with, "I think this is what God is saying, but I am open if you think it's not."

It shocked me when my usually non-emotional husband began to cry. "Sarah, He has already been speaking to me," he said. "I prayed He would speak to you." Caleb explained God had revealed His plan to him a few weeks before when he was in Southeast Asia doing mission work. He knew where we were supposed to go and with whom we were supposed to work. We were to live in Hong Kong and work in Southeast Asia, especially in Cambodia. He felt we were to help the pastor he had visited fulfill God's vision for that country. As He described what God had shown Him, I grew excited about our next season (though I also felt overwhelmed!).

That night, we prayed together and committed our path to God. We fasted for further direction, sought godly counsel, and then began taking steps of faith. As we did, God opened many supernatural doors of opportunity. Out of our time and relationships in that season, we went on to complete 31 children's homes, five schools, 170 water wells, and two churches, resulting in thousands of lives saved, healed, and restored. God performed miracle after miracle, but each miracle started with a moment of hearing His Spirit and responding in obedience.

I can tell you from experience that, as you seek the person of the Holy Spirit and focus on building your relationship with Him, everything else will fall into place. Priscilla Shirer put it this way: "Make knowing Him your goal. Seek a Person instead of a plan. Seek a relationship instead of a road map. The closer you get to God the more He will reveal Himself to you, and the natural result of knowing Him better will be a greater ability to discern His voice."[4]

HIS PEOPLE

The third way God speaks to us is through His people—through believers submitted to Him. Proverbs 24:6 (AMP) says, "For by wise guidance you can wage your war, and in an abundance of [wise] counselors there is victory *and* safety." Hebrews 1:1 says, "In the past God spoke to our ancestors through the prophets at many times and in various ways". . . and He still does today.

God will use people to speak something you need to hear—whether through sermon, a conversation, or even a pointed word of prophecy. It will always be a trusted individual grounded in the Word. The words they speak will line up with Scripture and will probably confirm something God has already been stirring in your heart. Romans 8:16 (AMP) says, "The Spirit Himself testifies *and* confirms together with our spirit [assuring us] that we [believers] are children of God." Their words will also ultimately bring peace, even if at first you feel overwhelmed.

> "Make knowing Him your goal. Seek a Person instead of a plan. Seek a relationship instead of a road map. . . ."—Priscilla Shirer

DREAMS AND VISIONS

The fourth way we hear God is through dreams and visions. Throughout the Bible, we read about God giving dreams and visions to Joseph, Daniel, Ezekiel, Paul, John, and many more. And He still gives them to us today! God uses visions and dreams to show us a picture of what's ahead. Acts 2:17 says, "In the last days, God says, I will pour out my Spirit on all people. Your sons and daughters will prophesy, your young men will see visions, your old men will dream dreams."

This is how God spoke to me in my encounter at 11 years old. In the vision He gave me, I was standing next to Jesus in a room filled with video screens. Pictures of children of all nationalities flashed across the screens. These children were obviously in great need—hungry, abandoned, and homeless. In the vision, I cried and asked, "Jesus, why are you showing me this?"

He replied, "Because these are the people I've called you to."

When I told Jesus I felt too young for this, He reminded me of Jeremiah 1:5. It says, "Before I formed you in the womb I knew you, before you were born I set you apart; I appointed you as a prophet to the nations." After that service, I wrote about everything I had just experienced. I tucked the journal away in my room, promising God I would go wherever He wanted me to. Later, I told my dad, and I'll never forget his response.

"Good!" He said. "I believe you will go to the nations, but don't wait! You can start here and now!" He helped me sign up for various projects in our church and community, and I served kids locally throughout the next decade. Now, over 30 years later, Caleb and I are fulfilling that vision through our work with children throughout Asia.

Friends, God has so much in store for you. He wants to speak to you in every season and situation. Will you listen? I encourage you to try it today. Listen, and when He speaks, identify what way He is using to speak to you. Then write what you sense Him speaking. Later, go back and read it. Ensure that what you sensed lines up with Scripture. Pray for confirmation, and if needed, pray for God to align your desires with His. Hold on to that word, believing it will come to pass. Remain open and expectant for further direction. And when you get it, obey quickly and fully.

We now know the promise of hearing from God. We recognize the ways we can hear from Him. Now, let's talk about what can keep us from hearing. Let's uncover hindrances that try to stand in our way.

Questions for reflection:

1) Is God first in your life? Is He your best friend? If not, what are you prioritizing above your relationship with Him? What are three ways you can better prioritize your relationship with God so that you hear Him more clearly?

_____

_____

_____

_____

_____

_____

_____

2) In what ways have you heard God before, whether or not you realized it was Him at the time?

_____

_____

_____

_____

_____

_____

_____

_____

3) As mentioned in the chapter, spend time listening today. When God speaks, identify what way He is using to speak to you. Then write what you sense Him speaking. Later, go back and read what you wrote, ensuring it lines up with Scripture. Hold on to that word, trusting God fully and taking the steps of faith necessary to do your part in making what He spoke come to pass.

_____

_____

_____

_____

_____

_____

_____

_____

_____

_____

_____

_____

_____

_____

Passage for further study:

1 Samuel 3

Prayer for today:

Father,
Thank you for the ways you speak to your people. Help me discern
your voice and the leading of your Spirit more clearly every day as I
continue to build my relationship with you. Then, help me hold onto your
promise, trusting you to bring your words to pass as I walk by faith.
In Jesus's name,
Amen

CHAPTER 3

REMOVING HINDRANCES

The word they heard did not profit them because it was
not united by faith in those who heard it.
Hebrews 4:2 (NASB)

L et's be honest: life is loud. Every day, thoughts, voices, ideas, and opinions fight for our attention. Some are the right ones, leading us further into what God has for us. But some only serve as hindrances along our journey. As we learn to listen for and obey the voice of God, we will have to learn to discern between the two. In previous chapters, we learned we all have access to God's voice. We also talked about the ways we can hear Him. In this chapter, I want to talk about obstacles that hinder us from hearing.

DOUBT

The first hindrance to hearing God is doubt. We read about it in James 1:5-8, which says:

> *If any of you lacks wisdom, you should ask God, who gives generously to all without finding fault, and it will be given to you. But when you ask, you must believe and not doubt, because the one who doubts is like a wave of the sea, blown and tossed by the wind. That person should not expect to receive anything from the Lord. Such a person is double-minded and unstable in all they do.*

We can boldly ask God for what we need; but when we ask, we cannot doubt. We must ask in full faith, knowing our Father will be good to us.

> Many times, we're looking for a big sign when God wants us to tune into the gentle whisper of His voice.

DISTRACTION

The second hindrance to hearing God is distraction. Each morning, we wake up to a list of notifications reminding us of all we have to do. We see the tasks that need done and the people that need cared for. Although these alerts might reflect good priorities, they still shouldn't come before God. We're to put Him first, taking time to listen for His voice and seek His wisdom. God will help us be more effective than we could be on our own! He has strategies, direction and creative ideas to propel the very things we're working on to the next level. He can show us how to be the parent, spouse, and leader He has called us to be, but we have to remove distractions. We have to push past the static and press into Him.

One day, I was traveling to preach in another city. My kids weren't with me, and I was honestly enjoying the alone time. I was strolling from shop to shop, reading magazines and browsing through stores, savoring the quiet. After a while, I noticed a line at my gate, so I joined it. Forty-five minutes later, I made it to the front of the line and handed the lady my ticket. She glanced at me, and then at the ticket. Then, she glanced at me again, and then at the ticket again. She did this a couple more times before asking, "Girl, are you paying attention? This line is for Jacksonville, Florida, and your ticket says Jacksonville, North

Carolina! You're at the wrong gate. You'd better run!" I did run—and *fast*! I had to catch a train to another terminal, but thankfully, I made it just in time.

This memory reminds me of how vital it is to pay attention in both our natural and spiritual lives. If we allow ourselves to get distracted, we might miss our destination. Like with my flight, the right way may not be initially obvious. We might not hear it called over the loudspeaker. Instead, we might discover it in a simple conversation with Jesus—so we need to pay close attention. Elijah was in this position in 1 Kings 19:11-12. Chaos surrounded him. He desperately needed direction, guidance, and encouragement. The passage says:

> *The Lord said, "Go out and stand on the mountain in the presence of the Lord, for the Lord is about to pass by." Then a great and powerful wind tore the mountains apart and shattered the rocks before the Lord, but the Lord was not in the wind. After the wind there was an earthquake, but the Lord was not in the earthquake. After the earthquake came a fire, but the Lord was not in the fire. And after the fire came a gentle whisper.*

Many times, we're looking for a big sign when God wants us to tune in to the gentle whisper of His voice. He has divine strategies, ideas, wisdom, assignments, and guidance for all areas of life. He'll give us vision, direction, and creative ideas. I've learned from experience—what's spoken in a gentle whisper can open doors of opportunity that eliminate years of struggle. But like Elijah, we must quiet ourselves both on the inside and on the outside.

Psalm 46:10 says, ". . . Be still and know that I am God . . . " In our culture, stillness is rare, but it's vital to hearing God. In a world of chaos, we must choose to live differently. Sometimes that means silencing our cell phones, deactivating our social media, or turning off the TV. Sometimes, it's taking a walk alone or waking up early for a moment of stillness. Whatever we have to do, we must ensure we are ready to hear God's gentle whisper.

DISOBEDIENCE

The third hindrance that can keep us from hearing God is disobedience which, many times, looks like procrastination. Sometimes, we aren't hearing because we haven't obeyed the last instruction He gave us! Isaiah 1:19 says, "If you are willing and obedient, you will eat the good things of the land."

Procrastination is sneaky. It can hinder people for years, so we must obey quickly and fully. If you feel stuck, take a moment to reflect. Has God asked you to do something you've put off? If so, waste no more time. I promise you—if you'll obey the step He has given you, the next one will become clear.

> What's spoken in a gentle whisper can open doors of opportunity that eliminate years of struggle.

SIN

The fourth hindrance is sin. Isaiah 59:2 (NLT) says, "It's your sins that have cut you off from God. Because of your sins, He has turned away and will not listen anymore." Sin dulls our hearing. To stay sharp, we must remain in the Word, allowing God to correct us, direct us, and adjust things in our lives. Remember, God doesn't correct us because He is a harsh dictator trying to make us into perfect robots. He corrects us for our own good, because He wants the best for us.

God doesn't stop at correction, though. He forgives and restores us, too. Romans 3:23 says, "For all have sinned and fall short of the glory of God." 1 John 1:9 says, "If we confess our sins, he is faithful and just and will forgive us our sins and purify us from all unrighteousness." No matter how many times we fall short, we can always approach God's throne boldly, requesting grace to meet us in our toughest times.

We'll never be able to change the past; we can only focus on our present to change our future. As we get serious about any sin in our lives—repenting and receiving God's grace—we'll hear more clearly. Thank God, His mercies are new every morning. Great is His faithfulness!

In our culture, stillness is rare, but it's vital to hearing God. In a world of chaos, we must choose to live differently.

BITTERNESS

The last hindrance is common and often hidden. It's bitterness, which is offense that has taken root in our soul. A root of bitterness keeps us from hearing God. It's why Jesus said in Mark 11:25 (NLT), "But when you are praying, first forgive anyone you are holding a grudge against, so that your Father in heaven will forgive your sins, too." Every day, we should ask God, "Do I need to release any unforgiveness to you? Is there anyone I need to make things right with?" He will always let us know.

When He leads you to eliminate hindrances, remember: anything He asks you to remove is for your good. He wants you to have His best.

Listen—I know forgiving is hard, especially when the person you're forgiving shows no remorse, but Jesus not only commands us to forgive, He also gives us the grace to do it (Mark 11:25). Forgiving others also benefits your own health, wellbeing, and purpose. Releasing that person and situation to God will help you move forward and will bring healing, freedom, and peace to your heart.

God *can* and *will* turn difficult situations around. When He leads you to eliminate hindrances, remember: anything He asks you to remove is for your good. He wants you to have His best.

Questions for reflection:

1) Take time to reflect. Are there areas in your life in which doubt is hindering you from hearing God? If so, write how. Then write the steps you need to take to remove that hindrance. Now, do the same with the other three areas: distraction, sin, and bitterness.

_____

_____

_____

_____

_____

_____

_____

2) Think back on your life. Try to remember a time when God was trying to speak through a gentle whisper. Did you miss it? If so, what were the ramifications? How can you ensure that doesn't happen again?

_____

_____

_____

_____

_____

_____

_____

3) If, in Question 1, you wrote about something that has hindered you in the area of bitterness, return to it. If you haven't already, pray a prayer of forgiveness. Release the situation and trust God to bring peace and vindication.

_____

_____

_____

_____

_____

_____

_____

_____

_____

_____

_____

_____

_____

_____

_____

_____

Passages for further study:

John 20:24-29; Luke 10:38-42; Isaiah 59:2; Hebrews 12:15

Prayer for today:

Father,
Thank you for leading me daily. Help me remove any hindrance that
stands in the way of that leading. Show me where I may be allowing
doubt, distraction, sin or bitterness to keep me from you. Then help me
rid my path of those hindrances so I can run fully into your purpose.
In Jesus's name,
Amen

CHAPTER 4

HOW TO KNOW GOD'S WILL

He wakens me morning by morning, wakens my ear to listen like one being instructed... The Sovereign Lord has opened my ears; I have not been rebellious. I have not turned away. . . Therefore, I have set my face like a flint, and I know that I will not be put to shame.

Isaiah 50:4, 5, 7 (NIV)

In the previous chapters, we discussed the promise of hearing God, the ways we hear Him, and the obstacles we face in hearing. So now, let's talk about what happens we hear Him, and how we determine if what we're hearing is really His will.

In my dad's book, *Led By His Spirit*, he said this:

In discerning God's will you need to first understand that God's will for you is good! He wants to:

› Save you (2 Peter 3:9)

› Heal you (1 Peter 2:24; Matthew 8:16;17)

› Empower you with the Holy Spirit (Acts 1:8)

› Bless you (Galatians 3:14)

› Protect you (Psalms 23)

› Preserve you (Psalms 121)

› Deliver you (Psalms 37:40, 91)

. . . Always remember where God guides, He provides. He won't tell you to do something and then ask you to do it in your own strength. He supplies everything you need through Jesus Christ."[5]

God wants to us to know His will because He loves us and wants the best for us. Still, when you sense God has spoken to you, it can be easy to wonder, *Was that God or me? Is this really what He is saying? Or is it just what I want?* In another book, my dad gave seven questions you can use to determine God's will. He taught them to me when I was young, and they have proven invaluable to my journey. I firmly believe they will be the same to yours.[6]

> "... Where God guides, He provides.
> He won't tell you to do something
> and then ask you to do it in your own
> strength."—Billy Joe Daugherty

JESUS

The first question is, "Will Jesus be glorified by my decision?" The Spirit will never lead us to do something that doesn't honor the Lord. When the Holy Spirit speaks, He always exalts Jesus. Practically, we can ask, "Does this person I'm considering marrying already exalt Jesus in their daily life? Does this business partner make decisions that exalt Jesus? Can I use this job to bring glory to Him?" When we can honestly answer *yes* to these kinds of questions, we know we are on the right track. We can go on to the next one.

THE BIBLE

The second question we can ask in determining God's will is, "Does this decision line up with the Bible?" As we mentioned earlier, Scripture is the ultimate authority. Hebrews 4:12 in the Amplified Translation says:

> For the word of God is living and active and full of power [making it operative, energizing, and effective]. It is sharper than any two-edged sword, penetrating as far as the division of the soul and spirit [the completeness of a person], and of both joints and marrow [the deepest parts of our nature], exposing and judging the very thoughts and intentions of the heart.

As we previously mentioned, just like a surgeon's knife cuts and divides flesh from bone, The Word has the life-changing ability to cut to the core of our inner being, dividing between soul and spirit. When we seek God through the study of His Word, it helps us discern between our feelings, emotions, mind, will and spirit. It brings direction to our season and clarity to our steps.

When Caleb and I were pastoring in Orlando, a couple received Jesus in a service. They started studying God's Word together and surrendering everything in their lives to Him. Until that point, they had been living together unmarried, but as they studied Scripture, they came across 1 Corinthians 6:13-14; 18-19. They realized their relationship was not honoring God, so they repented and decided to marry.

Our friends asked us to marry them, and we were honored to do so. It was an incredible moment to watch them surrender their union to God! As this beautiful couple kept allowing Scripture to direct them, God kept blessing them. Today, they remain strong in their faith and in their marriage. That's what God's Word does. It reveals the truth with supernatural grace and wisdom, changing our life for the very best.

The Spirit will never lead us to do something that doesn't honor the Lord. When the Holy Spirit speaks, He always exalts Jesus.

PEACE

This third question has proven invaluable to my life many times. It's the question of peace. When discerning God's will about a situation, we should ask ourselves, "Does this decision produce peace in my heart?" Colossians 3:15 (AMP) says:

And let the peace (soul harmony which comes) from Christ rule (act as umpire continually) in your hearts [deciding and settling with finality all questions that arise in your minds, in that peaceful state] to which as [members of Christ's] one body you were also called [to live]. And be thankful (appreciative), [giving praise to God always].

What does an umpire do? He calls the shots. He lets us know what's in and what's out. That's what the peace of God does in our lives. Ignoring God's peace can bring great trouble and heartache, but paying attention to it can bring lasting joy and success. Though I heard this truth often growing up, I didn't fully experience the reality of it until my college years.

Just before starting my freshman year of college, the Lord put on my heart not to date that first year. It made little sense to me, because I had dated a few guys in high school, and dating had never been a major distraction for me. I had been looking forward to getting to know new guys in college—guys that loved Jesus and wanted to serve Him. But the more I prayed about the decision, the more I felt God wanted my focus on what I already had going. I was a full-time student, worked a couple of jobs, was a children's pastor at our church on the weekends, and was the chaplain on my dorm floor. So, I committed to what God had asked.

The first semester went great. I met new friends, excelled in school, and found purpose in all of my activities. I loved how close to God I had become. When spring came along, though, I grew restless. As my friends started pairing up, I began questioning whether I had really heard from God. I asked myself, *What if I'm missing it? What if I'm missing the one God has for me?*

One guy had pursued me consistently throughout that first year, and it was wearing on me. He was popular, and a lot of girls wanted to date him. I concluded, "If I don't date him, somebody else will." I ignored the lack of peace and focused on the fact that he loved the Lord, and that spring, we started dating. We dated for two years, and then he asked me to marry him. I was so surprised! When he asked, I remember my stomach tightening up. I didn't have peace, but I didn't want to hurt his feelings, so I said yes. As our engagement progressed, I numbed this lack of peace with the excitement of planning a wedding and a new life together.

Thankfully, God intervened. Ten days before our wedding, my fiancé approached me with personal issues that had surfaced. We had a decision to make. He suggested postponing the wedding, but I knew we had to call it off. So, though the cake was made, the dress was altered, and the RSVPs were collected, I called off the wedding and, ultimately, the relationship. It was hard, and it hurt, but I'm grateful I followed through.

In the weeks that followed, I sought God fervently. I wanted to know where I had missed Him. His response was clear: at the beginning. He graciously showed me He had been trying to speak to me through a lack of peace from the start of my time in college and throughout the entire dating process. It was a tough realization to come to that though I felt close to Him, I hadn't trusted Him with my whole heart. I decided that day I would never make choices without Him again. I promised to follow His leading and peace, even when the matter seemed trivial or the answer made little sense to me.

About a year and a half later, my then-friend Caleb Wehrli began pursuing me. We'd been friends for a long time but had not been in a dating relationship. The first date we went on, he shared his dreams, vision, and calling in life with me. I will remember that moment forever. I listened in awe as he basically shared my own heart back with me. I didn't share my thoughts with him, but I felt peace about the relationship. I knew we were heading in the same direction.

Throughout the months following, I asked for and received confirmation of that peace. When Caleb proposed to me, I said yes with complete confidence. I knew I wanted to spend the rest of my life with him, chasing God and His purposes together. I'm so grateful that, though I learned the hard way, I ultimately allowed peace to be the umpire in my life. Caleb has been my best friend, the love of my life, and my husband for over twenty years now!

Philippians 4:6-7 reminds us, "Do not be anxious about anything, but in every situation, by prayer and petition, with thanksgiving, present your requests to God. And the peace of God, which transcends all understanding, will guard your hearts and your minds in Christ Jesus."

Friend, if you too will trust God with your whole heart—allowing His peace to guide your life—you'll forever be grateful you did. His plan is more beautiful than you could ever imagine.

When we don't know what to pray,
the Holy Spirit does. He always prays
in agreement with the will of God.

THE HOLY SPIRIT

The fourth question is, "Does the Holy Spirit bear witness with this decision?" As we said before, the Holy Spirit is Jesus's gift to every believer to help us navigate life on earth. We gain more insight about who He is and how He helps us through Scripture.

Romans 8:14 says, "For those who are led by the Spirit of God are the children of God." Jude 1:20 (GNT) says, "But you, my friends, keep on building yourselves up on your most sacred faith. Pray in the power of the Holy Spirit." Romans 8:26 (NKJV) says, "Likewise the Spirit also helps in our weaknesses. For we do not know what we should pray for as we ought, but the Spirit Himself makes intercession for us with groanings which cannot be uttered." When we don't know what to pray, the Holy Spirit does. He always prays in agreement with the will of God. How powerful!

In 2009, after Caleb and I had obeyed God's leading and moved our family to Hong Kong, we took a trip to Cambodia. On that trip, we held several outreaches, hosting a women's conference and dedicating a church we had just built. One evening, I went to the church for a meeting. When I walked in, I saw a bunch of kids sleeping on the floor, so I asked the pastor why. He explained the kids had nowhere else to go, so he allowed them to sleep there.

I instantly knew the Holy Spirit was leading me to do something to help these kids. When we returned to Hong Kong, I could not forget them. I continually prayed about what part I was to play in resolving their heartbreaking reality. It wasn't long before the Holy Spirit brought the answer: He wanted me to build them a home that would offer protection, provision, and education.

I was hesitant, as I'd built nothing like that to this point. I didn't know where to start, so I shared the prompting with Caleb. He encouraged and challenged me, saying, "Sarah, I have enough projects to believe God for. He spoke to you, so you're going to have to believe God for this. Get your faith out there and start taking steps."

That challenge was just what I needed. With Caleb's support, I started taking one step at a time. I wrote the vision, researched, and prepared. I found the right people and laid the framework. Finally, it came time to pay for the work to be done, and I had no idea how it was going to happen.

That same month, I was hosting a women's conference at our church in Hong Kong. As I prepared, I felt in my spirit to share the vision with the pastor. He was so moved by it, he asked me to share it with the women. Because this was not a large group, I thought little of sharing it with them. However, when I did, the women latched on to the vision. They gave toward the project and reached out to others to give as well. Within ten days, all the money for the home had come in. It was truly a miracle.

"When God calls you to do something, you can give yourself wholly to Him and expect Him to equip you. He may not confirm this up front, but as you take each step, more of His plan and His will will be revealed to you." —Oral Roberts

---

We built that first home in 2010, and 36 children moved in. For the rest of their childhood, these kids were clothed, fed, cared for, educated, and—most importantly—loved. Today, they are pursuing God's purposes for their lives. Some have received higher education, some have attended Bible school, and some have gotten married and started families. As of today, we have raised funds to build many children's homes throughout Southeast Asia. Now, hundreds of lives have been and are being impacted through the love, support, and care they have received.

Obeying that one prompting of the Holy Spirit has resulted in much life change for many people. That doesn't mean it was easy, though! Following through with God's will doesn't keep you from obstacles; it just helps you when you face them. God will always give you the grace and strength you need to press on.

> "The vision is yet for an appointed
> time . . . though it tarry, wait for it;
> because it will surely come. . . . "
> —Habakkuk 2:3 (KJV)

TIME

The fifth question is, "Am I making this decision in God's timing?" When we sense God leading us in specific ways, it's often wise to let time prove it's Him. Many times, people will tell me, "We need to do this right now." In those moments, I've learned to ask why. Usually, they respond, "Well, we have a deadline." I reply, "Who set that deadline?" Most of the time, it was us, and we can move it. Sometimes, it wasn't us, but if we talk to the ones who set it, they agree to move it. It's always better to let the dust settle until you can clearly decide with full confidence what God wants you to do and how He wants you to do it.

We should never push ourselves to get married, take a job, make large purchases, or other life-altering decisions. This is because under pressure, we can make wrong decisions. It's easy to act upon a flash idea in a moment of inspiration. But many times, this leads us onto a rabbit trail, and we end up in a ditch somewhere way off track! Later, we realize we never should have made that decision in a rush. Hindsight is always 20/20.

All throughout Scripture, we're told the importance of times and seasons. Habakkuk 2:3 (KJV) says, "The vision is yet for an appointed time. . . though it tarry, wait for it; because it will surely come." Ecclesiastes 3:1 (NKJV) says, "To everything there is a season, a time for every purpose under heaven." God wants us to trust His timing, even when it takes longer than we would like for it to take. It's not always easy, but it's always the best.

Answering the question of time works well because, as Psalm 33:11 (NKJV) says, "The counsel of the Lord stands forever." God's plans stand. As you are seeking God first for His wisdom, if something is really Him, He will increase the desire for it in your spirit. In his book, *Still Doing the Impossible*, Oral Roberts wrote, "When God calls you to do something, you can give yourself wholly to Him and expect Him to equip you. He may not confirm this up front, but as you take each step, more of His plan and His will will be revealed to you."[7]

WISE COUNSEL

The sixth question is, "What does wise counsel say about this decision?" Psalm 1:1 (NKJV) says, "Blessed is the man who walks not in the counsel of the ungodly." This question gives two main things to consider. First, before you seek counsel, know the spirit of the person with whom you are seeking counsel. Just because someone is older or in leadership doesn't mean they have a spirit of faith. We see this truth play out in the story of the twelve spies in Numbers 13.

In this story, we read about twelve leaders within the community of Israel, each from a different tribe. Moses had led them, along with the entire group of Israelites, to camp outside of the Promised Land. After 40 years of wandering, they were finally about to enter the land God had for them. The problem is that the land was already occupied. So Moses sent the twelve leaders as spies to scope out the situation and decide how to approach it.

When they returned, ten leaders came back with a negative report. In essence, they said, "It's impossible. We're so small compared to them. We can't do it." They might have been right in the natural, but they forgot we serve a supernatural God! Thankfully, two of the leaders—Joshua and Caleb—portrayed a different spirit. They spoke in faith, encouraging the people that, because of God's promise, they could possess the land. Sadly, those that believed the negative report of the ten leaders never walked into the Promised Land. From their generation, the only leaders with a spirit of faith who walked into their long-awaited blessing were Joshua and Caleb.

When seeking counsel, remember that, like the ten spies, some will speak out of their personal opinions. We must not consider counsel from those not grounded in faith in God, as they could lead us astray. Instead, we should seek wise, godly, faith-filled counsel from people like Joshua and Caleb, who want us to flourish in our God-given purpose. We should seek wisdom from those who are grounded in the Word and led by the Spirit.

The second thing to remember when choosing counsel is that the words of a counselor should not override any of the previous tests. This is because we are not to be led by people. We are to be led by Jesus, God's Word, the Holy Spirit, His peace, and His timing. While a wise counselor will direct you toward these things, an unwise counselor will try to control you, influencing you with their emotions. Of course, this does not apply to a parent-child relationship in which we must decide for our children. Until they leave our home, we are responsible to help them walk the right way.

Seeking wise, godly counsel is one of the best things we can do. It helps us receive confirmation and pushes us further toward God's purposes.

WILL

The final question we can use in determining God's will is, "In this decision, have I surrendered my will to God?" God has incredible plans for our lives, and the enemy knows that. It's why he'll tempt us with wrong desires that try to pull us from God's plans. It's also why Paul tells us in Galatians 5:16 (NLT) to "... let the Holy Spirit guide your lives. Then you won't be doing what your sinful nature craves." When we submit our entire being—body, soul, and spirit—to God, we can resist the enemy and overcome our fleshly desires.

Jesus showed us how to surrender our will in Luke 22, just before religious leaders captured him, put Him on trial, and crucified Him. Jesus knew the trouble that awaited Him, so He went to the Garden of Gethsemane to pray. Because He was fully God, Jesus was aware of the agony, pain, rejection, and suffering He was about to endure. But because He was fully man too, He didn't want to walk through it. In prayer, He was so torn between His flesh and His spirit that Scripture says He sweat drops of blood. This is a medical condition called hematohidrosis, which is induced by immense stress.

In Luke 22:42, Jesus prayed, "Father, if you are willing, take this cup from me; yet not my will, but yours be done." Jesus surrendered His will to God's, and He went to the cross for us, changing our lives and eternity forever.

Throughout your life, you will feel the same pulling. Though it won't be of the same magnitude, you'll sense the tug-of-war between your flesh and spirit. In those moments, every one of us will have to decide which one we will choose. To live in God's best, we must surrender our will to His, praying like Jesus, "Not my will, but yours be done."

Questions for reflection:

1) Ask yourself, *Do I really believe God's plan is the best plan for my life? Or do I think I can come up with something better on my own?* Be honest as you write your thoughts. If there are areas in which you struggle, find Scriptures that combat your unbelief. Write those verses and put them somewhere you will see them often. As you begin to truly believe God's plan is best, you will begin to discern His will.

_____

_____

_____

_____

_____

_____

2) Think of an area in which you are seeking God's will. Spend time praying about it. Then, ask yourself the seven questions from the chapter, one at a time, writing out your answers.

_____

_____

_____

_____

_____

_____

_____

3) Reflect on every area of your life. Is there any one in which you have not completely surrendered your will to God's? If so, write it down. Then, pray the prayer below, submitting your will to His.

_____

_____

_____

_____

_____

Passage for further study:

Ephesians 5:15-17

Prayer for today:

Father,
I want to submit my will to yours, because I understand you have good plans for my life. They are plans to give me a future, a hope, and an expected end (Jeremiah 29:11). I accept your plans and purposes. I receive your divine direction and destiny. Empower me with the Holy Spirit, Lord, so I will make wise decisions in line with your Word and Spirit, so others will be drawn into God's family through my witness.
In Jesus's name,
Amen

CHAPTER 5

THE REWARDS OF HEARING AND OBEYING

The golden rule for understanding spiritually is not intellect, but obedience.
Oswald Chambers[8]

We've made it to our final chapter. So far, we've confirmed our ability to hear God, and we've talked through various ways He speaks. We've uncovered hindrances, and we've discovered how we can discern His will. Now, I want to discuss the most exciting part! I want to talk about the rewards of hearing and obeying God.

ETERNAL REWARDS

There are both eternal and natural rewards for hearing God's voice and obeying His leading. The eternal rewards are the lives affected and destinies altered for eternity. In Acts 8:26 (NLT), we see an example of this. Philip had just finished a fruitful time of ministry when an angel appeared to him. The angel told him to go "Go south down the desert road that runs from Jerusalem to Gaza." Scripture tells us he immediately arose and went.

When he got there, Philip met an Ethiopian eunuch. This eunuch was over the queen's treasury and had eminent authority throughout his land. He had just returned from worshipping in Jerusalem and was sitting in his chariot reading the Book of Isaiah, trying to understand it. God told Philip, "Go near and overtake this chariot." Philip caught up with the eunuch and asked, "Do you understand what you're reading?" His answer was no, so Philip sat with him and explained it. Before the trip was over, the eunuch asked Philip to pray with him to be saved and to baptize him. History records that Ethiopia experienced great church growth after this, linking that growth to this Ethiopian eunuch.[9] Philip's obedience made an incredible eternal impact from just one choice.

NATURAL REWARDS

What a beautiful day it will be when we get to heaven and see the fruit of all our obedience! But as exciting as that will be, God wants us to enjoy a fulfilling life on earth too. That's why He also blesses us with natural rewards when we seek Him. We see proof of this in 3 John 2, which tells us God wants us to prosper and be in health even as our soul prospers. When we follow God, He promises us direction, provision, favor, strength, peace, fulfillment, protection, significance, and purpose.

The story of Abraham, the father of our faith, is one of the best examples of obedience producing natural rewards. In Genesis 12, God told Abraham to move himself and his family to a land He would show him. Notice: He didn't say a land He *had* shown Abraham; He said a land He *would* show him. I'm sure obeying without knowing was incredibly difficult, but because he did, when Abraham reached the land, he was immensely blessed.

In Genesis 26, we see God direct Abraham's son, Isaac, to a specific place as well. When Isaac obeyed, He sowed seed in famine and reaped one hundredfold in the same year! Years later, God directed Elijah to a widow. When he obeyed and went to her, she, her son and Elijah all received provision in their hours of great need.

Friends, when we too listen to and obey God's direction, we find favor, provision, and divine appointments. His direction might not make sense to us at first. The results might not either. You might think, *I feel like I obeyed God, but I don't see the fruit.* Don't grow discouraged. God *will* bring a harvest.

A few years ago, Caleb and I needed funds for a mission project. We had saved as much as possible, but it still wasn't enough. One day, God spoke to us to sow all we had saved into five ministries that were doing the same things we were believing for God to do through us. Sowing those seeds was an enormous sacrifice, but after we did it, God supernaturally provided above and beyond what we could have ever imagined—not only with finances but also with opportunities. He provided for the outreaches and also for our personal needs—an apartment, and a vehicle. I remember feeling so in awe of God's faithful, practical provision throughout that season.

God won't only do things like this for Abraham, Isaac, and Elijah, and He won't just do it for us. He will do it for you too, as you obey His leading. Our Father is passionate about guiding us into His best for our lives. He faithfully leads us step by step, day by day, as we tune in to His voice and take steps in the direction toward which He is calling us.

ON THE OTHER SIDE

To close out our time together, I want to circle back to a story we've discussed throughout this book. It's the story of our trip to Cambodia—the one in which I encountered the kids sleeping on the floor and was inspired to build them a home. One thing I haven't mentioned is how hesitant I was to even go on this trip. See, just before we were scheduled to leave for it, my father passed away. We were living in Hong Kong and had traveled back to our hometown, Tulsa, Oklahoma, for the funeral. I didn't want to go because I felt I had nothing to give. I was exhausted and heartbroken, and I wanted to be alone.

After the funeral, I pulled my mom aside to talk to her about it. I told her all about what we had planned to do there and how I felt I didn't have the emotional capacity to go. Then I asked her what she thought I should do. Her response surprised me, though her wisdom did not. With grace, my mom reminded me of when Jesus discovered John the Baptist's beheading in Mark 6. He gathered the disciples, and they traveled across the sea so Jesus could be alone and rest. However, when they arrived on the other side of the sea, they realized they weren't alone. Thousands of people were waiting to hear from Him.

~~~~~~

There are always people on the other side of your obedience.

~~~~~~

Scripture says when Jesus looked out over the multitudes, it deeply moved Him to compassion. Instead of searching for another quiet place, He stayed and taught the people. When they grew hungry, He performed one of His most well-known miracles, turning a little boy's five loaves of bread and two fish into enough food to feed over 5,000 people.

After the story, mom answered my question. "Sarah, do you realize a miracle happened amid Jesus' loss? I know you're grieving the loss of your father, but think of the multitudes of precious people in Cambodia who need the hope you have in Jesus. I believe if you'll reach out with the love of God, simply offering Him what you have, God will do miracles." After prayer and consideration, I knew she was right. I couldn't give up, because there were people on the other side of my obedience. So, I followed through with our plans, praying for God's grace and strength all the way.

~~~~~~

"It's not my ability, but my response to God's ability, that counts."—Corrie ten Boom

~~~~~~

What I didn't expect to happen was that, while I was in Cambodia ministering, joy flooded my heart, as if I was being reawakened to my purpose. Many received salvation, healing, and deliverance. While there, God also reminded me of the vision He had given me at 11 years old, to care for His children around the world. The vision for our first children's home was born out of that trip, and only a year later, the home had been built. In one of the worst moments of my life, God turned things around for good, using me to bring hope to others.

The best part about this story is that God is no respecter of persons. What He has done for me, He can and *will* do for you. But you first have to respond in obedience. Corrie Ten Boom said, "It's not my ability, but my response to God's ability, that counts."[10] Friends, if you too will trust and obey God, He will redeem even the hardest of seasons, using them for His glory.

Questions for reflection:

1) Think back to a time you obeyed God. What were the natural rewards? What might the eternal rewards be?

_____

_____

_____

_____

_____

_____

_____

_____

2) In what area has God already spoken to you, and how do you need to obey His voice? Write down as many areas as you can. Then next to each, write one step you will take this week to move forward in obedience. Remember that, often, God will not reveal the next step until we take the first one.

_____

_____

_____

_____

_____

_____

_____

_____

3) Take a moment to remember a time someone positively impacted your life for Christ. Maybe it was a parent, a grandparent, a pastor, or a friend. Ask yourself, *What would have happened if they had not been obedient to God's leading in their lives?* Then pray the prayer below, committing to obey God's leading so you too can impact people—both on earth and for eternity.

_____

_____

_____

_____

_____

_____

_____

_____

_____

_____

_____

_____

_____

Passage for further study:

Hebrews 10:35-36

Prayer for today:

Father,
Thank you for making your will known to me. Please give me the wisdom,
grace, and strength to obey, even when it's hard. As I do, I trust you will
continue to make your path known to me. I commit to walking that
path, knowing there are people on the other side of my obedience.
In Jesus's name,
Amen

APPENDIX A

Prayer of Salvation

If you would like to ask Jesus to be your Lord and Savior, I invite you to pray this prayer with me:

Jesus,

Thank you for your gracious gift of salvation. Thank you for your gift of eternal life in heaven and abundant life on earth. Today, I confess with my mouth that you are Lord and believe in my heart that you were crucified, buried, resurrected, and now sit at the right hand of the Father. Today, I renounce every work of darkness and accept you as my Savior. I'm grateful for the gift of eternity with you and for a life on earth I could never experience without You.

In your name I pray,

Amen

Congratulations! You just made the most important decision you'll ever make. You've changed your life and eternity forever! I know this all might be new to you, and you might have questions or need help getting started on your journey. If that's the case, we would love to help. Just send us an email at <u>info@ sarahwehrli.com</u> and let us know about your decision! We will rejoice with you and guide you in taking your next steps. Again, congratulations, and welcome to the greatest family you'll ever be part of!

APPENDIX B

Promises and Encouragement for:

Hearing God's Voice, Knowing His Will and Obeying His Leading

Deuteronomy 13:4 (ESV)

"You shall walk after the Lord your God and fear him and keep his commandments and obey his voice, and you shall serve him and hold fast to him."

Psalm 85:8

"I will listen to what God the LORD says; he promises peace to his people, his faithful servants—but let them not turn to folly."

Matthew 7:8

"For everyone who asks receives; the one who seeks finds; and to the one who knocks, the door will be opened."

Luke 11:28

". . . 'Blessed rather are those who hear the word of God and obey it!'"

John 5:30 (NLT)

"I can do nothing on my own. I judge as God tells me. Therefore, my judgment is just, because I carry out the will of the one who sent me, not my own will."

John 6:63

"The Spirit gives life; the flesh counts for nothing. The words I have spoken to you—they are full of the Spirit and life."

John 8:47

"Whoever belongs to God hears what God says. The reason you do not hear is that you do not belong to God."

John 10:2-5

"The one who enters by the gate is the shepherd of the sheep. The gatekeeper opens the gate for him, and the sheep listen to his voice. He calls his own sheep by name and leads them out. When he has brought out all his own, he goes on ahead of them, and his sheep follow Him because they know his voice. But they will never follow a stranger; in fact, they will run away from him because they do not recognize a stranger's voice."

John 14:26

"But the Advocate, the Holy Spirit, whom the Father will send in my name, will teach you all things and will remind you of everything I have said to you."

Romans 10:17 (ESV)

"So faith comes from hearing, and hearing through the word of Christ."

Hebrews 2:1 (NLT)

"So we must listen very carefully to the truth we have heard, or we may drift away from it."

Hebrews 3:15

"As has just been said: 'Today, if you hear his voice, do not harden your hearts as you did in the rebellion.'"

James 1:22

"Do not merely listen to the word, and so deceive yourselves. Do what it says."

1 John 5:14

"This is the confidence we have in approaching God: that if we ask anything according to his will, he hears us."

Revelation 3:20

"Here I am! I stand at the door and knock. If anyone hears my voice and opens the door, I will come in and eat with that person, and they with me."

ABOUT THE AUTHOR

Sarah Wehrli is a dynamic speaker and author, passionate about connecting people to their unique purpose and helping them experience God authentically. She has served in multiple areas of church leadership at Victory Church in Tulsa, Oklahoma, and has helped pioneer a church plant and mission projects around the globe.

Besides speaking, writing, and serving the local church, Sarah has an immense passion for missions. She serves as the Executive Director of Inspire International, a mission organization that focuses on evangelizing the lost, equipping leaders, and bringing practical relief to orphans and children at risk around the world. Sarah has ministered in 45 different countries over the past two decades, even serving with her family as a missionary in Hong Kong for a time.

Sarah has a theology degree from Oral Roberts University. She lives Tulsa with her husband, Caleb, and their three children: Isaac, Elizabeth, and Emma.

BOOKS AND ONLINE VIDEO MASTERCLASS COURSES

Awake

Have you ever wondered what your purpose is? Have you asked God what He put you on earth to do? Scripture says *you* have a specific destiny only *you* can fulfill. So it's vital to God's kingdom that you walk in your assignment! Sarah talks about this in *Awake*. Through stories, Scripture, and implementable action steps, she helps you awake to your divine assignment and rise out of anything trying to hold you down. You are alive at this point in history for a specific reason. You were born for such a time as this!

Advance

Have you ever felt stuck? Stuck in pain? Bitterness? Disappointment? Comparison? Fear? Shame? Do you want to move forward but don't know how? In *Advance*, Sarah teaches us how to live unstuck so we can advance in our walk with God and in the purpose He has for our lives. Through personal experiences, biblical principles, and practical tips, she addresses topics such as moving from comparison to confidence, fear to faith, confusion to clarity, discouragement to hope, surviving to thriving, and more.

Find these books, courses, and more at sarahwehrli.com.

Stay Connected

📷 @sarahwehrli   ⓕ @pastorsarahwehrli   🐦 @sarahwehrli

🌐 www.sarahwehrli.com   ✉ info@sarahwehrli.com   ▶ Sarah Wehrli

Request an Event

Women's Events
Conferences
Weekend services
Workshops
Online Events
Retreats
...and more

If you would like to connect with our team to discuss Sarah speaking at your service, event, conference, or gathering, email us at info@sarahwehrli.com

INSPIRE INTERNATIONAL CURRENT PROJECTS

Children's Homes

Inspire International builds quality homes for orphans and vulnerable children around the world. We help meet their physical, educational, and spiritual needs through partnerships with local missionaries, churches, and other established ministries.

Conferences and Outreaches

We conduct annual conferences and outreaches focusing on equipping leaders and empowering women to recognize their potential and value. In many village outreach projects, we partner with local ministries, providing resources to help those in need. Inspire also works with leading global ministries focusing on completing the Great Commission in our lifetime.

Water Wells

With the help of our partners, Inspire International builds family and community water wells that provide clean, reliable water in needy regions of Southeast Asia. In most places, these wells are the most reliable source of clean water the villagers have.

Education and Schools

Inspire International is dedicated to bringing the Word of God and the message of salvation to children throughout the world through education and school building projects. We accomplish this through partnerships with local missionaries, churches, and other established ministries.

Fighting Human Trafficking

We partner with organizations to help rescue women and children from predators by easing the burden of poverty and supporting ministries who are making a difference.

Church Buildings

Inspire International constructs church buildings around the world to give believers a place to worship together and to help strengthen the body of Christ.

Connect with
Inspire International

🌐 www.inspireintl.com

📷 @_inspireintl

👤 @InspireIntlMinistry

✉ info@inspireintl.com

ENDNOTES

1 Priscilla Shirer, *Discerning the Voice of God: How to Recognize When God Speaks* (Nashville, TN: LifeWay Press, 2017), 17.

2 "Preparing to Hear God's Word," *Bible.org*, accessed October 20, 2022, https://bible.org/article/preparing-hear-god%E2%80%99s-word.

3 Elisabeth Elliot, *On Asking God Why: And Other Reflections on Trusting God in a Twisted World* (Grand Rapids, MI: Fleming H. Revell, 2006), 126.

4 Priscilla Shirer, *Discerning the Voice of God*, 112.

5 Billy Joe Daugherty, *How to Know God's Will* (Tulsa, OK: Victory Christian Center, 1991).

6 Billy Joe Daugherty, *Led by the Spirit: How God Guides and Provides* (Orlando, FL: Creation House, 1994), 14-15.

7 Oral Roberts, *Still Doing the Impossible: When You See the Invisible, You Can Do the Impossible* (Shippensburg, PA: Destiny Image, 2002), 210.

8 Oswald Chambers, "The Way to Know: July 27," *My Utmost For His Highest*, accessed October 19, 2022, https://utmost.org/classic/the-way-to-know-classic/.

9 Elesha Coffman, "What Does History Say about the First Christians of Africa?" *Christianity Today*, August 8, 2008, accessed October 20, 2022, https://www.christianitytoday.com/history/2008/august/what-does-history-say-about-first-christians-of-africa.html.

10 Steve Gladen, *Small Groups with Purpose: How to Create Healthy Communities* (Grand Rapids, MI: Baker Book House, 2013), 17.

CPSIA information can be obtained
at www.ICGtesting.com
Printed in the USA
JSHW021023090223
37482JS00004B/23